Purpose

God Has a Plan

Rosemary Singleton

Savannah, GA

Published 2024
Printed in the United States of America

ISBN-13: 979-8-218-3667-6-6 (print)
ISBN-13: 979-8-218-3667-7-3 (e-book)

Editing and book design by Rebekah McKamie and Settings Christian Publishing, LLC

Cross book image: © abstract – stock.adobe.com.
Black line image: © Rezual -stock.adobe.com
Licensed for use by Rosemary Singleton

The author has obtained all necessary permissions to reproduce all photographs within this work.

Scriptures taken from the King James Version (KJV). Public domain.

O taste and see that the LORD is good:
blessed is the man that trusteth in him.
Psalm 34:8

And we know that all things work together for good to them that love God, to them who are the called according to his purpose.

—Romans 8:28

According to the Bible, our purpose, the reason we are here, is for God's glory. In other words, our purpose is to praise God, worship him, to proclaim his greatness, and to accomplish his will. This is what glorifies him. Therefore, in this, we find that God has given us a reason for our existence. . .We were created by him, according to his desire, and our lives are to be lived for him so that we might accomplish what he has for us to do. When we trust the one who has made us, who works all things after the counsel of his will. . .then we are able to live a life of purpose.

—Matt Slick, founder and president of carm.org

Contents

Contents

Acknowledgements

I would like to thank my husband, Bishop Calvin N. Singleton, and our children: Calvin N. Singleton Jr, Clarence Singleton, Tabitha Singleton-Atkinson, and Malachi Singleton.

Special thanks to my nieces Tissany Chatman and Sarinaty Labrew; and to my daughter's friends Sherron Adams and Mary Christine Agengo for their inspiration through our conversations.

Special thanks to my church family, which has always been there to help me, encourage me, and pray for me.

In memory of my parents, the late Inez and Alton Nealy, who I love and will never forget I come from; my sister Kathy Nealy, my oldest sister and friend Carolyn, and her husband Phillip Chatman.

And thanks to all my siblings Alton Nealy Jr., Christine Nealy, and Tammy Nealy.

Introduction

"The LORD of hosts hath sworn, saying, Surely as I
have thought, so shall it come to pass; and as I have
purposed, so shall it stand."
Isaiah 14:24

The thought of writing a book came to my heart off and
on for about ten years. On three separate occasions within
the ten years, guest speakers at my church said that the
Lord showed them I would write a book. At those times I
could not see it, but I knew the thought had crossed my
mind. I would try to start writing and did not know where
to begin and then I would stop and not try again for a
while. I did not know how it was going to happen and I was
waiting to hear from God. I thought to myself, if God
wants this then God will bring it forth, because I had no
clue how to write a book.

There were times I would try to write but ended up
writing only a sentence or two, not knowing where to go
from there. I felt stuck and confused. Still, I would try
again. Toward the end of the year 2022 my heart was
leading me again to start to write. I was still trying to figure
out where to start and what to write about and what
direction to take. Would this be one subject or more?
Would it be about pastors' wives, my family, all women, or
me?

One evening as I was sitting at my computer, I heard a
voice in my heart telling me to start typing whatever came
to my mind—whatever thoughts I had. And that's what I

Contents

did. There were always thoughts running through my mind, so I started to type my thoughts. I did this over and over. Then after several weeks of typing and reading what I wrote, I noticed that certain things went together that were the same subject, so I started moving things into categories. I realized these could be chapters and I continued to do this.

I realize now that I wrote this book because I wanted to tell my story—something I have been feeling for some time. I could feel the urging in my heart to tell the story of how God had a plan and a purpose for me and my family even before I knew it.

On my life's journey, I have learned that God has a way of teaching us what he wants us to know. He wants us to know He is there, He does hear us when we call, He does care, and that He is able to work it all out for our good. I have learned that God will allow some unpleasant things to happen in our lives for our benefit, for the benefit of drawing us closer to Him, for the benefit of teaching us about what He can do, and for the benefit of growing stronger in Him. This helps us to get to know Him and experience Him working in our lives. Through it all, we become witnesses of His goodness and of His power.

"God is our refuge and strength, a very present help in trouble" (Psalm 46:1). The Lord was my help in time of trouble. I know He brought me through many things, and He kept me. He kept my mind.

I want wives and mothers and all women to know that God cares about us, that God does work in our lives, and that He does have a plan for us even if we don't know it yet. I am a witness that the Lord does care about us. He has proven it to me over and over again.

Chapter One

The Beginning

I met my husband, Calvin, at church one Sunday morning. As he came in, my pastor greeted him. At that moment, my sister and I were walking past, and my pastor called us over to introduce us to Calvin. We were the first people my pastor introduced him to. I was in the sixth grade at this time.

I later learned that Calvin, along with his mother and aunt, lived in town, but they were members of a church that was out of town. Calvin said he passed by my church one day and went home to tell his mother that he would like to visit the church. So, they all visited my church on a Sunday evening when I was not there. Calvin told me that after evening service my pastor introduced himself to the guests, and they all said that they enjoyed the service. He invited them to come back. Calvin told me that after attending service he asked his mother if he could join our church and she said he could. After this, Calvin became a member of our church.

Through conversation with Calvin, I learned that he was in the fifth grade and went to a different school than I did. One day at church he asked my mom if she could pick him up for midweek church service because his mom worked at night. This meant I would see him at least twice a week. It almost feels like we grew up together, and I guess we did.

As we were growing up, our church had many teenagers. We all hung out together, and it was fun. About six of us went to the same high school, so some of us would have lunch together. We would also walk home together, laughing and talking as we walked. Some of us even became best friends.

I liked Calvin as a friend. I got to know him as time went by, and we participated in church activities in groups. We had church youth sessions, we went on bus trips to an amusement park, and we hung out together at the city park. We went to different churches with our pastor who would treat us all to McDonald's. Calvin and I would talk and have fun together during these activities.

Calvin was always a friendly person; well-mannered and liked by everyone. People always had good things to say about him. They would say he was a good kid; he had good manners, he was good at sports, he was helpful, and he was a good worker. Calvin kept jobs while going to high school. People even said that he would be a good husband for someone one day. My parents liked him as well, and they spoke highly of him. And as I got to know him better, the things that people said about him I found to be true.

Calvin was also well-known. One reason he was well-known is because his mother was a beautician and had lots of customers, which included some women from our church. He played the guitar and sang in church. He also was well-known because he played football and was the undefeated heavyweight champion in wrestling during high school. I remember riding the city bus one day and hearing some people talking about him. They were rooting for him to win his wrestling match.

I did start to have feelings for him; I remember feeling a little tingle in my heart. I kept this to myself. That tingle is what made me decide to go see him at his wrestling match. My sister Carolyn went with me to the match. Calvin noticed us there and asked us to wait for him so we could walk to church together for the midweek Bible study night. So, we waited for him.

Sometimes my sister and I had friends from church over to our house and everybody would sing while Calvin and others played music. In my family of six siblings, three of us could sing and three of us could not. I was one of the three who could not sing. I did sing in the church choir but could not sing alone or lead. This is so funny because I was always singing or humming to myself. The three siblings that could sing inherited it from my mother. She loved to sing, and she loved it when we got together like this. Growing up, our family even sang along with the TV commercials.

Fast forward, on the day of my graduation from high school in June 1974, I was walking home with another young man from my school who was also a member of our church. This young man had been trying to get my attention for a little while now. So, I decided to talk and listen to what he had to say and to find out what kind of person he was. As I talked and listened to this young man, I decided that we would remain friends and nothing more.

When I got home, my sister told me that Calvin had called. Before I could call him back, he called again and asked if he could take me out for dinner to celebrate my graduation. I said yes, I would enjoy that, and I looked forward to it. We then agreed on a time for him to pick me up. He took me to a very nice Chinese restaurant, and we had a wonderful time together.

I truly enjoyed Calvin's company. He was genuine and truthful and a great conversationalist. He was not the type of person to play the little games young men played. Young men play these games where they would say something to you to see what your response would be and see how far they can get or go with you. He was not trying to get something from me or pull something over on me. He was just nice and pleasant and friendly.

After a couple of weeks, we were still going on dates together. I realized that these dates were turning into a different kind of relationship; we were becoming more than friends hanging out. The day came when Calvin asked me to be his girlfriend. I told him that I would let him know. I could see in his eyes that he was a little disappointed. After a week of not responding to him, Calvin called me and said he would ask me one more time. If I did not respond, he would go his way and not bother me again. What made me hesitant, even though I did have feelings for him, was the fact that Calvin was a year younger than me. While I was graduating from high school, he was still in school. But after Calvin's phone call, I knew I had to make up my mind. I knew that I really liked him, and I knew despite him being a year younger than me that he was a very mature person. So, I had to decide whether I wanted to take this chance with a younger guy or not. I finally said yes that I would be his girlfriend. From then on, we were together a lot, not only as a church group, but as a couple.

At first, I remember wondering what the reason would be for our breakup. I thought that because I was out of school and about to go to college, I would look foolish dating a guy that was younger and still in high school. But after a few months I realized that nothing was going to break us up. I genuinely enjoyed being with him.

During the summer of 1974, we talked about everything. But when Calvin started talking about marriage, I was a little stunned—no, not stunned—I was not ready for this conversation. In fact, I was upset about this conversation. I told him that I was not ready to marry anyone. Despite not being ready to talk about marriage, we kept seeing each other. It got to the point that we saw each other every day, and before long we were inseparable and very much in love. By Christmas of that same year, we had been together for six months when Calvin asked me to marry him.

I said yes, and I was very happy, excited, and in love. As I look back, this all happened fast, and I now believe it was part of God's purpose and plan for our lives: "A man's heart deviseth his way: but the LORD directeth his steps" (Proverbs 16:9).

I was happy, but I wanted to be sure I was making the right decision, because I knew getting married was nothing to take lightly. I remember asking the Lord if I was making the right decision. I asked myself if I absolutely loved this man or was I in love with the fact of getting married. I asked the Lord to show me if I should marry him. I weighed the thought in my mind and prayed until the answer from my heart came. I was not marrying this man because I wanted to get out of my parents' house. I was not marrying this man because I wanted someone to take care of me. I knew I loved this man. Also, what helped me make my decision is the fact that I knew this man. I knew his character. We talked a lot about everything. It's important to talk and get to know each other; it helps to make wise decisions.

I remember my aunt asking me if I really wanted to get married so young. I did not answer her. But I realized that Calvin and I were both mature people for our age and we knew exactly what we wanted. We were not forced into this; we did not have to do this. But we loved each other, and this is what we both wanted to do.

We soon began planning our wedding, which would take place two years and eight months from December 1974. Every paycheck I earned went toward the wedding until everything was paid for. Calvin contributed to our wedding, and he also saved and paid for our honeymoon trip, furniture, and our first apartment.

Before we knew it, two years and eight months had come. But on August 5, the day before our wedding, I had a car accident. My dad had gone out and bought coffee for him and my mom that morning. They drank two different kinds of coffee. When he left the house to go to work, he grabbed the wrong coffee. My mom insisted I take his coffee to him. I did not want to go; I told my mother that he probably threw away the coffee he had and already started working. But she kept insisting that I take his coffee to him. While driving, I spilled coffee on myself. I looked down in my lap and ran into a car on the other side of the road. I had my three-year-old niece with me. I saw blood on her and was frantic; I started checking to see if she was alright. She was fine. The blood on her was from me! I did not realize it, nor did I feel it, when I hit my chin on the steering wheel.

The ambulance and the police came, and we went to the hospital. The emergency room checked my niece for injuries; thank the Lord she was not hurt. Someone called my sister, her mother, at work and told her what happened. She dropped everything and sped to the hospital. She checked on her daughter, the hospital released her, and they went home. I had to have stitches in my chin and was released. After I came out of the emergency room, I realized that I did not have a car and there was no one waiting to take me home. I called my mother and the first thing she said was, "How is the car?" I got so upset that I hung up the phone. I never, ever would do that to my mother. But she did not ask about how I was doing or if I was alright. She was only concerned about the car—my father's car. I called a taxi to get home.

By the end of the day, Calvin came to the house to see me, not knowing what had happened. As he walked into the house and toward me, I had a newspaper up in front of my face so he could not see until he got closer. I put the newspaper down and I showed him my chin. It was swollen, and you could see the stitches. I remember one of my sisters asking me if I was still getting married. I replied, "Of course I'm still getting married tomorrow!"

The car accident was not the only difficulty that occurred. On the day of the wedding, all the bridesmaids were at my house getting dressed as the photographer took pictures. One of the bridesmaids broke the heel of her shoe while she was coming down the stairs. My mom told my youngest sister to take it to the shoe shop, which was only a block away. My sister did not like this idea, and did not want to do it, but she did. Then the cars that were supposed to take the bridal party to the church did not show up. So that meant we had only one car for five bridesmaids and me. We all piled into one car and drove to the church. The matron of honor and her husband drove their car, and the flower girl rode with her parents to the church. After we arrived at the church and all the bridesmaids got out, I was sitting in the car waiting for the wedding director to come get me for my time to walk down the aisle. Someone came to tell me that the best man, Calvin's brother, forgot the ring. But it turns out that Calvin never gave his brother the ring and he was the one who forgot it. That felt like the last straw, as they say. I was about to cry, but then noticed that people were peeking in the car window at me. They wanted to see the bride. We used my oldest sister Carolyn's wedding ring for the ceremony, and it worked out fine.

After the ceremony, we went to the park to take pictures, which was relaxing and exciting at the same time. It was relaxing because after taking some pictures the photographer told me to sit down on the grass and relax. I was so tired, and I relaxed my body while he was taking pictures of the bridal party. I did not realize he was also taking pictures of me sitting there on the grass and being so relaxed my back was hunched over. It was also exciting to see the photographer taking pictures of my bridal party.

The Beginning

While I was watching, it hit me: this is surreal! I was now a married woman. This was a momentous day.

Relaxing in the grass.

After taking pictures, we headed to the banquet where the reception was being held. It was stunning as we walked in and saw all the guests sitting at the beautifully decorated tables. We were enjoying the reception until the DJ started playing music we did not approve of. Calvin was upset and was about to go say something to the DJ, but I told him to let it be. We also noticed that there were people at the reception that were not invited. Later, the maître d' came to us and said that other people had come late and there were no more chairs to seat them. He asked if we wanted to set up another table. I looked to see who the people were, and I was heartbroken when I saw that they were the guests we had invited. We decided to have the maître' d set up another table, which cost us money. Earlier that day we paid for everything in full, so we did not bring a check or cash with us. I took the money out of my bridal bag—a white satin money bag that the bride carries as she greets her guests. They give her wedding cards which contain monetary gifts. We had to use these gifts to pay the maître d' for the other table.

After the situation with the table, we had a wonderful time. Then we did something that shocked our parents. We planned to go home to our separate parents' homes instead of spending the night together. My parents laughed and asked if I knew what I was doing. I said of course I know what I'm doing. I wanted our first night together to be at the honeymoon location with all the frills of a honeymoon suite. When I talked to Calvin, he said his mother, grandmother, and aunt all laughed and laughed. Calvin told me that his aunt was laughing so hard she almost fell off the chair. To tell the truth, we both forgot we had an apartment already set up—a fully furnished apartment. One of us could have stayed there.

I remember when I got home after the reception, I tried to keep my wedding dress on as long as I could because it made me feel so beautiful. After hours of wearing it, I was so tired. When I could not take it any longer, I finally took it off and fell into my bed.

The next morning, I woke up not feeling well and did not know what was making me feel like this. The only thing I could think of is that this came from the car accident. I had a slight headache and my body felt like it did not want to move; I just felt so much discomfort. My mother suggested that I should not go on my honeymoon. She said I would not enjoy myself. When I called Calvin and told him I was not feeling well, we both decided not to go on our honeymoon. I later called the honeymoon resort and explained to them about the car accident and how I was feeling. They said to send a letter of explanation and they would return our deposit to us.

That morning, Calvin came to pick me up from my parents' home and we went to our apartment. When leaving my parents' home, Calvin told them that he was going to make breakfast for me (he was a great cook). My father was laughing and said, "Boy, don't you spoil that girl." We laughed and got into the car, heading to our new apartment.

The Beginning

Then began our life together as husband and wife. Now, looking back, it seems like we began our lives together and it took off running and never stopped.

After months passed, one afternoon I went to visit my parents and my father said something to me that I had no idea of what he was talking about. He used an old word from back in his time. I cannot remember the word he used, but I had to ask my mother what it meant. She told me it meant that I was pregnant. I responded in disbelief, but I soon found out it was true. I still wonder how my father knew. What did he see in me that indicated I was pregnant? But it was true, whatever he saw.

Within five months of marriage, I was expecting our first child. Then a year and half later we had our second child. Then in another year and a half came our third child. We had three children for thirteen years and then came our fourth child. Yes, thirteen years later. We had talked about having a fourth child several times years earlier, but it did not happen for us. I remember our daughter, Tabitha, would ask us for a baby sister and my husband would tell her that we were going to order it from the Sears catalog. How funny!

During this time, the thought of not being able to get pregnant never entered my mind. I just assumed it had not happened to me yet. As time passed, I realized that I had not conceived any more for some reason. But thirteen years later, I did get pregnant.

Life got busy as I started taking care of children, taking care of our home, working a job, and doing all the necessary and demanding things to take care of my family.

Even though we had some unexpected things happen on our wedding day, and even with all the responsibilities and busyness of family life that followed, there was a purpose and a plan for me, my marriage, and our family.

Chapter Two

Real Life Sets In

God had a purpose for my family. That was something I started saying. No, at first I started feeling it. It was many years into my marriage when I started to recognize this feeling.

At the beginning of my marriage, I was simply happy. It felt like I was living in a fairy tale. But real life sets in fast. I had to learn what being married really meant. Now we had to pay bills. We had to put our money where it needed to go and not just spend it on ourselves. Now I was learning how to consider someone else before making decisions by myself. I learned that marriage is about two people, not just one person, and that things would not always go my way.

My husband and I came from different homes with different teachings and different ways we do things. In marriage, we must learn how to join our differences and work together to manage our new life. Marriage is learning to compromise and do the things needed to keep it going in the right direction and make it all work.

In a marriage, learning to communicate and to hear each other is very important. I have learned that we can both speak the same word but have two different meanings of that word. It takes time to build that understanding, so it is important to keep trying and having conversations. Marriage is about loving and caring for each other, appreciating what each person does in the marriage, and telling each other that you appreciate and love them. I know that through praying and asking God for help, and with the guidance of the Holy Spirit, a happy marriage is possible. But it takes work from each spouse. Marriage is not one-sided; it cannot work if only one person is working at it. Both persons must be in it for the good of the marriage.

I remember thinking about all the things a wife and mother does in her home. It can be overwhelming at times. I remember feeling tired and saying that I was "just a housewife." But being a housewife and mother is a very important responsibility.

Society tries to say that being a housewife or a stay-at-home mom is not important and that you are not working. But we are working, and it is meaningful. I said that if cooking, cleaning, ironing, and washing clothes is what helps take care of my family, then I will be a housewife. I told myself I will do what I must to take care of my family, no matter what society says.

I thank God for my husband; he is an extraordinary person. He worked hard and never complained. He always said, "A man does what a man has to do to take care of his family." He said with the help of the Lord, he would be able to take care of us and make sure we had what we needed as a family.

Yes, I had my challenges in this life, in marriage, raising children, dealing with finances, dealing with health, and dealing with people. John 16:33 says, "These things I have spoken unto you, that in me ye might have peace. In the world ye shall have tribulation: but be of good cheer; I have overcome the world." God never said life would be easy, but He said He would be there to help us through it, and this the Lord did for me.

When I started having that feeling that God had a purpose and a plan for my marriage and family, I really did not know what the purpose was, even after years of marriage. I just knew God had a plan.

I was expecting our first child within five months of marriage. I did not think much of it then, but when I think now of how fast this happened, it amazes me. I now realize that God knew what He was doing in my life, and I do believe the Lord knew each of our children and what they were to become. It seemed fast for us, but this was the right time for our first child to be born so he would be who God intended him to be and fulfill the plan God had for him. And the same is true for our second child, our third child, and even our fourth child.

As it says in Jeremiah 1:5, "Before I formed thee in the belly I knew thee; and before thou camest forth out of the womb I sanctified thee, and I ordained thee a prophet unto the nations."

At the time of my fourth pregnancy, I was in total denial. I was working as a secretary for a communications company and every day I went to work and got sick. I wasn't throwing up, but I was feeling awful. I remember I would come into my office, open my computer, and then go to another office where I knew no one would come in. There, I would lay my head down on my desk and then stretch my body over the desk. I would call my husband and tell him that I was sick. He would tell me go home, and

I would cry to him, "I can't, I have to work." I would lay on that desk for a few more minutes and then go back to my office and begin working. I started to notice that I was putting on weight and had to wear my blouse on the outside of my skirt because it made me look smaller. I kept saying, "I don't know what is wrong with me." The thought that I might be pregnant never entered my mind because I thought I could not get pregnant.

Then one day I decided to go to my primary doctor to have a checkup. I explained to him how I was feeling. He asked me a lot of questions and I answered them all. He said, "If you say you're not feeling well, we are going to find out why."

During the doctor's examination, it came time for me to take a chest x-ray, but the doctor asked me some more questions and then said he would not be able to do the x-ray. The last question he asked me was when my last cycle was. I told him that I could not remember and insisted that had nothing to do with this. The doctor replied, "You could be pregnant, and we cannot do the x-ray." I totally ignored what he said because I had not been pregnant in thirteen years, and I assumed that I could not get pregnant. I got so upset when he would not do the chest x-ray. I wanted to know what was going on in my body and why I was sick every morning. The doctor completed his examination by taking blood and urine from me and said that they would give me a call when the tests were done.

A few days later, while at work, the doctor's office called me and the nurse said,

"Congratulations, your test is positive!" I replied in a stern voice, "Positive what?" Then she said, "You are pregnant." When I heard those words, I felt my mind scrambling to understand what the nurse was talking about. I immediately hung up the phone—no, I slammed the phone down—because I was confused. I did not believe what I had just heard. I did not comprehend what this nurse was saying, and thought she got it wrong. I then decided to call and make an appointment with my gynecologist.

In the next week or so, I went to my gynecologist and explained to her how I was feeling. I told her about the visit to my primary doctor and the chest x-ray that the doctor would not do. I also told her about the nurse who called to tell me that I was pregnant. I told her that I knew I was not pregnant.

She said in her Asian accent with a chuckle, "Sooo Rose-ma-rie, you don't believe you are pregnant." She then told me to lay down on the examination table. She took the stethoscope, placed it on my stomach, and listened to it. The doctor then proceeded to put the stethoscope in my ears. She said, "Rose-ma-rie, do you hear that?" I said in a concerned voice, "Yes, what is wrong with me?" The doctor smiled and said, "That is your baby's heartbeat." I remember in a quick second I swallowed, clearing my throat, and I was feeling a bit confused. Then I said in a calm, low, slow, one-word-at-a-time voice, "That's—my—baby's—heart—beat?" The doctor also told me I was almost four months pregnant.

I was stunned. I couldn't believe it. But this time I accepted it because I heard the proof in my baby's heartbeat. After this, my mind was blank, and I moved in slow motion.

Chapter Two

When I got home and told my husband, he was ecstatic. This is the man who said he wanted six children when we first got married. Now it was time to tell the children, who were sixteen, fourteen, and thirteen years old. I was a little embarrassed to tell them. I felt at thirty-eight years old I was too old to be pregnant and at their ages they knew what it took to get pregnant.

That evening, my husband asked the children to come into our bedroom because we had something to tell them. When the children came in, I couldn't bring myself to tell them, so I quickly told them to get out. Yes, I said, "Get out." Then I said to my husband that I must do this before someone else tells them. So, Calvin told them to come back into the bedroom again. Before I could say anything, our oldest son broke out crying. He said he thought I was sick. I assured him that I was not sick, but I was expecting a baby.

Our second son blurted out, "Why did you and Daddy not use condoms?" I tried to ignore him, but he said it three times. I said to him, "If you say that one more time, I'm going to wring your neck." Our daughter, who was thirteen years old, was silent for a minute. I guess this had to sink in and then she was happy. She was so excited she asked me if she could call Mama, her paternal grandmother, to tell her the news. I was crying and said in a loud voice, "No!" But she asked me again and I said, "Yes, call your grandma."

I sat on the bed, still crying. My husband sat down beside me and asked what was wrong with me and why I was crying. I shouted, "Leave me alone!" And he did just that; he left me alone. He went downstairs, and I was trying to get myself together.

All I could think of at the time is that I was starting over: baby crying, baby bag, baby formula, changing diapers, up all night, no sleep and not being able to get up and go when I wanted to. Plus, I was thirty-eight years old.

That evening I told my youngest sister, who was living with us at the time, the good news. When I told her, she said that she already knew because I would come into the house every day from work yelling at the kids to turn on the air conditioner and the kids would reply, "Mommy, the air is on."

The next day, I called my parents and told them I was pregnant. My father yelled in the background, "Don't you have a television set?" Meaning, "Can't you find something else to do?" That really hurt me.

My mother said, "You almost have six kids." And I responded with a sarcastic tone of voice, "You mean like you do?" After this I just didn't feel much like anything. I needed something to cheer me up. The next day I went shopping and saw this beautiful black sequin "full" dress. It had bright-colored rhinestones on the collar. It was not a maternity dress, but I really liked it, so I bought it. I can see that dress in my mind right now. After that I went to get my hair done.

On Sunday morning, I got dressed and went to church with my family as usual. I was feeling some-kind-of-way, so I sat in the back of the church instead of my normal second row seat. Before the service was over, a lady from our church sent me a note. I opened it and it read, "You look so beautiful. You look like an angel." Well, that did it

21

for me. I was no longer feeling some-kind-of-way. I then started telling people I was expecting.

My emotions still got the best of me. I remember my husband had a speaking engagement at another church, so we all boarded the bus. Instead of me sitting in the front, like normal first ladies do, I decided to go sit in the last seat at the back of the bus and dared anyone to sit next to me. I was so moody; I couldn't help myself. This is too funny.

Soon everyone knew I was expecting a baby and people were happy for me. They were congratulating me and asking when the baby was due. As the months passed, I was getting bigger and bigger. My church family gave me a baby shower and we had such a great time.

I remember going for a checkup and taking my daughter, Tabitha, with me. The nurse was doing the ultrasound and had the transducer, the instrument used to place on my stomach to check the baby. As the nurse was moving around the transducer, she was talking about the baby and said, "It looks like it's a boy." As she said that, I quickly looked at Tabitha and tears were flowing down her face. She wanted the baby to be a girl because she still wanted a little sister. The nurse saw Tabitha's face and tried to change her words by saying, "It could be a girl; we have some time before we know for sure."

Again, the Lord had a plan and purpose for my life and my family. The Lord gave us this fourth child, born thirteen years after our third child, for a purpose. God has a plan for this child as He does for the other three. Psalm 127:3–4 says, "Lo, children are an heritage of the LORD: and the fruit of the womb is his reward. As arrows are in the hand of a mighty man; so are children of the youth." All four of our children were a part of God's purpose for my life and family, and I am grateful for each of them.

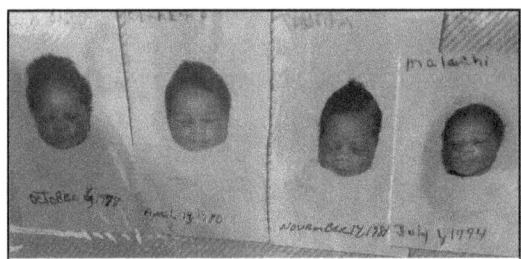

Calvin Jr.–1978, Clarence–1980, Tabitha–1981, Malachi–1994. Each time I gave birth, I felt a great responsibility.

Chapter Three

Family Life

My husband and I have now been married for forty-four years as I write this. One day we were home alone, which made us think about when we were first married. There was no one in the house but us. Our first two sons are married and have children of their own. Our daughter has been living on her own for quite a while, and our youngest son is still living with us, but he was out on this particular day. We were sitting there talking about our life together and how young we were when we got married and thanking God for His goodness. We started reminiscing about our children and some of the funny and not so funny things that happened in our family.

I remembered Calvin Jr., our first child, who walked at seven months old. One Sunday after church service, we were home making dinner and had the radio on, listening to gospel music. He loved music, so he tried to get to the radio and walked over to it.

I screamed, "He's walking!"

His daddy came into the living room to see, and Calvin Jr. did it again; he walked to the radio. When we were out at the grocery store or mall, people would ask us all the time how old he was, because he was so little to be walking.

From there, we started to remember many incidents and challenges with our first child.

Calvin Jr. was about a year old when he had a fever, and we could not break it. We tried everything. We called the doctor, and he gave us a prescription. We filled the prescription and gave Calvin Jr. the medicine, but it did not break the fever. We finally took him to the emergency room, and they could not break it either, so they kept him in the hospital. One day in between me leaving the hospital and Calvin coming, they wrapped our son's entire body in cold sheets without our permission. After that, Calvin Jr. was afraid of anyone who wore white, but the fever broke.

We remembered when we bought Calvin Jr. a toy guitar. He took it to church with him and sat in the first row with his paternal grandmother (Mama). The next Sunday, all the little boys had guitars and sat in the first row too.

My husband reminded me of another incident that happened when I was taking a night class and left the children with him. Calvin Jr. was playing with his rubber alphabet pieces and got one stuck in his nose. Calvin told me that he had a tough time getting it out. Calvin was about to call the ambulance, but he finally got it to fall out of our son's nose.

Calvin Jr. was three years old when his sister was born. Once, my friend came to visit, and I was downstairs with her. While we were talking, Calvin Jr. came downstairs and muttered words I thought were "see the baby." I replied, "The baby is sleeping. You can see her when she wakes up." And he went back upstairs to play, I thought.

My friend asked if she could see the baby. I said yes, and she went upstairs. When she got to the top of the stairs, she froze and started screaming my name. I rushed upstairs and saw the baby with Calvin Jr. on his bed, hanging halfway off the bed. This scared us. I ran to get the baby before she fell to the floor. At that time, we had

Clarence, one year; Tabitha, six months; Calvin Jr., three years

hardwood floors. Calvin Jr. had gone into my bedroom, taken the baby out of the bassinet, carried her to his bedroom, and put the baby in his bed. This little boy was too much.

That reminded me of another time when I was late picking Calvin Jr. up from school. When I got to the school, he was not there. I asked the teachers where he was, and they said he had left already. Apparently, the teacher assumed his parents were outside waiting as they let the children go. I was so upset and scared. During this time, we had only one car. Calvin drove it to work, so I usually walked to pick up Calvin Jr. from school, which was only four blocks away. For some reason I was late that day. I was walking with one baby in the stroller and my other son holding onto the stroller. So, I walked back home to see if he had walked home, but he was not there. I got really scared at this point and I was asking myself where he would go.

Family Life

As I was praying, asking the Lord to help me, I thought about my mother because she lived closest to the school. I then walked to her house and there he was. I asked him how he got there. He said he walked. I asked him how he crossed the streets. He said that the crossing guard helped him. I was so puzzled as to how he knew how to get to my mother's house from school. When I asked him, he said he remembered the way we drove to her house. He really scared me that day because he was only in the second grade. I was never late again.

This reminds me of the story of Mary and Joseph when they were returning home from Jerusalem. I can imagine how they felt when they could not find Jesus. They had to stop and look for him. I am sure they were frightened and worried just like I was until they found him (Luke 2:41–48).

When Calvin Jr. was sixteen years old, he came to my office at the church and asked me a question. He said, "Mommy, what does the Lord have for me to do? Clarence plays the organ, but what am I going to do? How is the Lord going to use me?" I told him that I did not know, but the Lord would show him. As his mother, you would think that I had some idea of how the Lord was going to use him, but I had no idea at all.

As time passed, my husband had Calvin Jr. help him make phone calls to set up dates, times, and travel arrangements for guest speakers for different church events. He was good at this, and my husband said that people would tell him how polite and professional Calvin Jr. was. The Lord used Calvin Jr. in this manner.

Chapter Three

Later, Calvin Jr. also became a minister. Now he is a preacher of the gospel and a pastor. I never saw this coming. He is an amazing man of God who preaches and teaches the Word of God with clarity and relevance. He coined the phrase "Victory is my only option," and it has become a strong declaration in our church. It exemplifies a strong word of testimony for us. I am amazed at how the Lord is using him. He is also an amazing husband and father who cares for his family. God has a purpose and a plan!

As we sat in the family room that day Calvin and I began talking about our second child, Clarence. I remember he was nine months old, and he was very sick. Just like the time with Calvin Jr., I called the doctor, and he prescribed some medicine. But the medicine did not help, so we took him to the hospital. They said that he had a fever, and he was dehydrated. As soon as they hooked him up to the intravenous, his face plumped up, and he started feeling better.

Because Clarence had been walking for a few weeks now, he did not want me to hold him. He wanted to get down off my lap and walk around. The nurses wanted to know how old he was and said he was so cute.

One day when I was potty training Clarence, I was in the bathroom with him while we were singing and clapping until he used the potty. I had to run to my bedroom to get something. Clarence got off the potty, closed the bathroom door, turned the lock on the door and locked himself in the bathroom. I tried and tried, but I could not unlock the bathroom door. He was crying, and I was crying. I tried using a knife to unlock the door, but it did not work. I was trying to think fast about who I could get to help me. I thought about my friend who lived around the side of the building. I ran to get her, and she unlocked the door by using a knife. I guess it did not work for me because I was nervous and scared. Anyway, Clarence was free, and we were all happy.

We talked about when Clarence was five years old, and he had an ear infection. The pediatrician gave him medicine, but his ears would not unclog. So, the doctor sent us to a specialist. The specialist looked at Clarence's ears and said that his ears were closed, and he might need to have surgery to unclog them. I told the doctor that we would hold up on the surgery and see if Clarence's ears would open with the help of medicine. So, he gave us a prescription for Clarence's ears. When we got into the car, I told Clarence that we were going to pray for his ears to open so he would not need to have surgery. I prayed first, then Clarence prayed for his ears to open. When it was time for Clarence to go back to the specialist, the doctor checked his ears and said one ear had opened. I said, "Thank you Jesus." I told the doctor that we would wait for the other ear to open. Again, when it was time to go back to the doctor, the other ear was also opened without surgery. Clarence and I both thanked the Lord for his healing.

I remember when Clarence was about ten or eleven years old, and it was his turn as a chore to sweep the kitchen floor after dinner. Clarence was always playing around. He was singing and swinging the broom around in the air. I said to him, "Stop swinging the broom around and sweep the floor before you break my hanging porcelain ducks." I went upstairs and after about fifteen minutes I heard a noise that sounded like something fell and smashed to pieces. Sure enough, Clarence broke my hanging ducks.

Clarence was a slim little boy with very skinny arms and legs. He used to wear socks that came up as high as his knees. One day, Clarence decided he wanted to build up his muscles and put on weight. He asked his dad to buy

Calvin Jr, four years; Tabitha, one year; Clarence, two years

him barbells. Clarence got the barbells, but his dad told him not to lift too often because it would stunt his growth. We later asked the doctor about the barbells stunting Clarence's growth, he said that is something parents believed but it is not true; it is a myth. He began lifting weights and he eventually built up his muscles. Then he started showing everybody his muscles. He was so proud of himself.

Clarence started learning and playing the organ at the age of seven. We had a small organ in our dining room, and I remember sitting down one evening and showing Clarence the C major scale on the organ and he repeated what I did. When my husband came home, I told him that Clarence picked up the scale fast. My husband sat down on the organ with Clarence and showed him some notes and Clarence repeated it. My husband was so excited and played more notes, and again Clarence repeated it. He kept playing more notes and Clarence kept repeating them. Then, with excitement, my husband said, "I think this boy is going to play this organ." And in God's purpose and plan, Clarence became a skillful musician, songwriter, music director, and producer. He has written and produced songs for several well-known artists. One of the songs he produced is entitled "Triumph." It is a great song with great lyrics and great music. Clarence has also become a husband and father who cares for his family dearly.

As we were still reminiscing about our family, we started talking about Tabitha, our third child and only daughter. We remembered Tabitha had started trying to walk, but she would only stand. We could see on her face that she was trying to figure out if she could take a step. On this day, she stood up and started bouncing up and down, still trying to figure out if she could take that first step. We could see on her face that she was afraid, but she finally took that first step and started walking. She was ten months old, and we were so excited. Then I remembered as Tabitha got a little older, she only had brothers to play with, so she wanted toy trucks. I remember her grandmother bought her a cabbage patch doll, and she hated it. She would say, "I do not want that bald-headed doll." So, we went out and bought her a barbie doll with extra doll clothes and a barbie doll pool. She played with the doll and clothes for a little while, but what she really liked to play with was the pool. That lasted for a little longer, then she stopped and decided to play with the trucks again.

Another thing that stuck in my memory is when Tabitha was about ten years old and she told me that she did not like hair bows and frilly socks anymore. I was a little hurt, but I realized that she was getting older, and changes were happening. I once tried to convince her to buy a new Christmas barbie doll and in her little girlie voice she said to me, "Mommy, I don't want one, but you can buy one for you." That was her polite way of saying she didn't want it! I also remember when she wanted to do her own hair, and I walked past the bathroom one day and she was combing her hair. Instead of easing the comb through the tangles, she was snatching her hair, breaking it off. I showed her how to ease the comb through her hair without breaking it off.

I remember telling Tabitha that soon it would be time to shop for a bra. She told me she would never need a bra. I just said okay, because I knew better.

As Tabitha was growing up, she sang in the church, and she also sang in school. In school, she became known as the singing girl. Tabitha sang many times in school and was accompanied by her brother Clarence on the piano. I remember this one time when she told me she was doing a solo for a school concert. Her paternal grandmother, Mama, bought her this pink dress, and she was beautiful. What I did not know was that an entire orchestra was accompanying her—it was amazing. She also sang in the church choir and later became a praise and worship leader.

Tabitha became an exceptionally good cook. She cooked for events at the church. She wanted to graduate from high school, go to college to become a chef, and then get a job as a chef on a cruise line and travel the world. Later, she changed her mind about being a chef and went into multimedia and web design. After returning from college, she began working for a bank, and later became a project manager and a scrum master. This was agile project management—a person who facilitates the work performed, especially by eliminating obstacles to the completion of tasks and achievement of goals.

Tabitha is a compassionate person. She enjoys participating with her church in helping distribute blankets, water, diapers, and food to the people of the city. She is also a wedding planner, which she is great at because she is very resourceful and thinks thoroughly through every detail. She was ordained as a minister, and her first sermon was entitled, "I can't see it, but I can hear it." What a great sermon. I was so proud of her. In her growing up days, I did get a glimpse of knowing that she may preach the Word of God. I was listening to her talking one day, and in my heart, I could hear her preaching the

Word of God. But I never told her what I saw. Tabitha became a strong woman and a wonderful wife. She is a caring person who enjoys cooking and having her family and friends over for dinner. God has a purpose and a plan!

As we continued to reminisce, we started talking about our fourth child Malachi, born thirteen years after Tabitha. I remember when we brought Malachi home from the hospital his three siblings were so excited. He was like a babydoll to them. They were amazed by this little person who was their new baby brother. When they all came home from school, Malachi would be asleep, and they would ask why he was always sleeping. They wanted

Malachi, six months

to wake him up, but I said no, let him sleep, he is growing. As time passed and Malachi began to crawl, they would get so excited watching him. They loved their little brother.

I also remember when he was about a year old, and he was in Tabitha's bedroom. Somehow, he got a little jingle from his tambourine stuck in his throat, and Tabitha was screaming. We ran into her bedroom and saw Malachi gasping for air. Calvin grabbed Malachi, put his head down on the bed and then put his finger down Malachi's throat to get the jingle out. That was so scary! We then took him to the emergency room to be checked, and the doctor said he was alright and that his throat was very red. We were so happy and grateful to God that Malachi was alright that day.

One day Calvin Jr., Clarence, and Tabitha had candy and decided to give Malachi chocolate when he was only a year old. They were not thinking that the chocolate would make him hyper. But when Malachi ate the chocolate, it did make him hyper. He kept getting up and running into the wall knocking himself back and falling to the floor and laughing. He did not hurt himself, but I told them not to give Malachi chocolate anymore. I also remember Malachi was in Tabitha's bedroom watching the movie Titanic and tears started flowing down his face. I didn't understand how a one-year-old little boy could be emotional about a movie.

One night when Malachi was about six years old, I put him to bed and went downstairs. I came back upstairs to check on him, and he was still awake. I asked Malachi why he was still awake. He replied, "I cannot go to sleep, Mommy, because I am thinking." I laughed and asked what a six-year-old could be thinking about. He said, "I don't know, Mommy, I'm just thinking."

Chapter Three

He was such a happy little boy. His kindergarten teacher told me that Malachi had a smile that lights up the classroom. She also told me that she knew he had older siblings because of his vocabulary.

Malachi, two years

I remember Malachi at an early age spending a lot of time with Clarence at the church, practicing music. One Sunday after service, I was walking up the stairs from the banquet hall and heard music coming from the sanctuary. I knew Clarence, who was our church organist at the time, had left the church. But as I was coming upstairs, I was wondering who was playing the organ because it sounded just like Clarence playing. When I reached the sanctuary, I saw it was Malachi playing the organ. I was so amazed. At this time, Malachi was only in the fourth grade. I did not know he could play like that.

Malachi grew up, went to high school, played football, graduated, and went to college. He grew up loving music and became our church organist and music director. He also started writing songs and creating music of his own. He wrote a song entitled "Destiny." It was a beautiful and encouraging song letting us know that we can do anything with the help of God.

Malachi was our last child to get married. We are grateful and proud of the man and husband he has become. God has a purpose and a plan!

Time goes by so fast, but I remember our children at different stages of their lives. I remember they participated in an Easter program at the church—their ages were six, four, and three. They recited the entire chapter of Psalm 23: "The Lord is my Shepherd." They were so cute. Often, we took them to the park and then to McDonald's for lunch, and I watched them eating and talking and enjoying their little lives.

In my mind I can see Calvin Jr., Clarence, and Tabitha running around and playing together in the backyard. I remember I would go to the back door to look out and check on them, and they would be having so much fun.

One Christmas when they were little, among their gifts they each had an instrument. These gifts were not wrapped, so they went straight for them. Calvin Jr. had a small guitar and amplifier, Clarence had a small drum set, and Tabitha had a tambourine. They were so excited, they ran to their instruments and started playing church, making a lot of noise. They were laughing and singing, jumping around, and having a good time. After they got tired of the instruments, they decided to open their other gifts. What a fun day that was.

When Malachi was born, his siblings were teenagers and they loved Malachi. As a baby, they would watch him, talk to him, and smile at him. When Malachi started crawling and walking his siblings would be watching him with excitement, they would scream out, "He is crawling!" When they saw Malachi walk for the first time, they would scream out, "He is walking!" As I tell these stories I can see them now.

I remember I had to stop Clarence and Calvin Jr. from watching wrestling on TV because they tried a wrestling move on their little sister. I went upstairs to check on them, and when I looked in their bedroom, Calvin Jr. and Clarence had their little sister turned upside down. They each were holding her by one leg and her head was hanging down toward the floor. I thought they were going to bounce her head on the floor like they watched the wrestlers do on TV. I quickly told them to put her down, and not to do that again, because they could drop and hurt her.

On another day, a Sunday afternoon, we were at Calvin's mother and aunt's house. All the adults were in the kitchen talking about how awesome the Sunday church service was. All the children were outside playing. Calvin Jr., who was eight years old, came into the kitchen and mumbled something about keys. I thought he was asking for the car keys, and I told him he couldn't have them, so he went back outside. Next thing I knew, someone ran into the house yelling that our car was rolling down the driveway. My husband ran out of the house and jumped over the ledge, trying to stop the car from rolling. We were truly blessed by God that day because there were no children outside, and usually the neighborhood children were outside playing. The car rolled down the driveway and across the street into a neighbor's hedges. Clarence was six years old and was in the driver's seat, the door was open, and he was shaking like a leaf. His eyes were big, and wide open. Calvin Jr. was standing in the driveway looking like he did not know what was happening and we could see on his face that he was scared too. After my husband got Clarence out of the car and drove it back into the driveway, we made sure that they were both okay and not hurt. Then we asked them what happened.

The questions that were quickly flooding my mind were: how did Clarence get the car in reverse, how did he get the keys, and how did he start the car? He was so little; you could not see his head over the dashboard. Clarence was a soft-spoken, quiet little boy who usually did not get into things he shouldn't. But sometimes he would follow his big brother and do what Calvin Jr. told him to do. We all knew this was not Clarence's doing. We asked Calvin Jr. about this; he said he came into the house and took the keys while all the grown-ups were talking. He told Clarence to get in the car, he put the key in the ignition, and pulled the gear down. That was a very scary day but thank God they were not hurt.

Not only did Calvin Jr. orchestrate this, but a few weeks later, he also told his friend, who was our next-door neighbor, to go in the house and get his mother's car keys. The little boy did what Calvin Jr. told him to do and when his mother came outside and saw him in the car, she started yelling at him and telling him to get out of the car. All the while, once again, Calvin Jr. was standing there looking like he did not know what was going on.

But despite all the amusing and scary things my children have gotten themselves into, they have grown up to be responsible and wonderful people.

Today the Lord has allowed my husband and I to see each of our children be used by God in an awesome way. I am grateful to God that they chose to live for Him. As it says in John 1:12: "But as many as received him, to them gave he power to become the sons of God, even to them that believe on his name."

I am a proud and grateful mother.

As we were still talking about our family, we remembered some of the tough times we went through.

I remember when we had only two children—one in the stroller and one walking on the side holding onto the stroller. I was out walking looking for a part-time job and decided to stop by my mother's house. As we were talking, she asked what I was doing today. I told her I was looking for a job. She asked why I didn't put the children in day care and then look for a job. I thought about doing that, and I just couldn't put my children in day care. I later told my husband that I was looking for a job, but I couldn't put our children in day care; I just couldn't do that. So, he said that he would get extra work along with his full-time job so I could stay home with the children. I was blessed to stay home for seven years taking care of our children. I deeply appreciate my husband.

Thinking back, I remember when we decided to buy our first home. We started looking at houses and came across one that we liked on the outside and was in our price range. We went to look at the inside of the house and I hated it. My husband asked me what I thought about the house, and I told him that I did not like it and didn't want it. He said to me, "Rose, this is what we can afford. I will make this house beautiful for you. Please say yes, and I'll fix it up and it will be beautiful. I promise you it will be beautiful." It took me a little time to think about it and I eventually said okay. Sure enough, he did exactly what he said he would do. We worked on the house until we got it where we wanted it to be—it turned out beautiful. I have an amazing husband. My husband has always made things happen; he has always accomplished what he set out to do. When things got tough, he kept going until he accomplished what needed to be done.

In the year 2008, the economy hit a slump. The job market was bad; jobs were few. After Calvin's place of employment went out of business, he started going out looking for employment every day, but could not find work. It was so bad we stopped putting our clothes in the cleaners, and I stopped going to the hair salon every two weeks and started doing my own hair. We even saw people in our neighborhood packing up their things and leaving their homes. We were months behind on our mortgage, but my husband kept going and he kept praying. One day on his employment hunt, he got hired and started making money. This was not the only tough spot we went through, but I can say that no matter what we went through, he never gave up or gave in. Calvin always had a determination to make it—to succeed. He was a very strong person and he always put his trust in God. He would say that God will make a way.

As my husband and I sat there in the living room reflecting on our life together—on our family and the years

God brought us through—we saw that God truly did make a way. After Calvin was blessed with employment, we were able to pay up our back mortgage payments and do other necessary things. The Lord did not allow us to lose our home, and He kept us in good health. As Calvin said, "God will make a way." The Lord did that. He made a way for us. Isaiah 43:15–16 says, "I am the Lord, your Holy One, the creator of Israel, your King. Thus saith the Lord, which maketh a way in the sea, and a path in the mighty waters."

God is so good.

Chapter Four
Not My Normal

The day my breast cancer story began was a freezing, wet, snowy, slushy day—the kind of day you do not want to go out at all. I had a mammogram appointment, but because of the weather I was debating with myself whether to go out in the cold or not. But deep down, my heart was telling me I should go. I finally decided to go, and I thank the Lord I did. He guided me to go because it saved my life.

I arrived at my mammogram appointment. I remember feeling so good to get inside the building and out of the cold weather. The technician told me to do the usual things like go into the room, take off my top, put the gown on, and wait for someone to come get me. Once inside, I was to stand close to the machine and they would take the x-ray on one side, switch to other side, and we would be done. When they were finished with the mammogram I would go back to my room and change back into my clothes and go home. There was no waiting and no other test to do. Normally, when everything went smoothly, it would be finished, and I would go home. But today was different; today was not my normal routine mammogram.

Here is where normal became not normal:

Not normal #1: The technician asked me not to get dressed after the mammogram.

Not normal #2: The technician said to wait in the waiting room after I did the mammogram.

Not normal #3: I was waiting too long for the technician to come back.

Not normal #4: The nurse, not the technician, came in the waiting room, and said they wanted to do a sonogram.

As I was sitting there waiting to hear something from the nurse, my mind started wandering and all kinds of thoughts came through my mind. Why did they have me waiting? What was going on? What did they see on the mammogram? Do I have cancer? I was remembering my mother when she found out that she had breast cancer. She had surgery to remove one breast and had to take a month or two of radiation treatments. I started feeling my anxiety level rising, to the point that I burst into tears. One of the nurses walking past the waiting room saw me and tried to comfort me. She said, "Mrs. Singleton, you are jumping the gun too fast, we just want to get a closer look. Do not worry." She eased my mind a tiny bit, but I knew this was not normal.

Finally, the other nurse came in and told me that they wanted me to do a sonogram for a closer look at my breast. When I finished the sonogram, they told me to make an appointment to see my doctor. None of this was normal.

I went home and I did not tell my husband or anyone else about this. I also felt ashamed. I thought that I let God down by not putting my trust in Him. My first thought was not, "Lord, I thank you because whatever is wrong, I know you will fix it, and everything will be alright." No, my first thought was, "I have cancer!"

I made an appointment to see my primary doctor. As he was doing his routine exams, checking vitals, heart, blood pressure, etc. he told me that he had received my charts from the mammogram. He proceeded to give me the name of a radiologist and told me to call and make an appointment. This was not my normal.

I finally went to see the radiologist and took more x-rays. The nurse told me the same thing the first nurse did at my mammogram appointment: "Sit in the waiting room. Do not get dressed yet. I will be back for you." Again, while in the waiting room wondering what was going on, I knew this was not routine.

The nurse came back to get me and led me into the office where the doctor was standing looking at a big screen. I noticed the nurse holding a box of tissues and I wondered why. Then the doctor said, "Mrs. Singleton, your x-ray is on the screen. As I point to the screen, I will explain it to you." He pointed to the screen and said, "This is calcium, and our bodies need calcium, but the problem is when they cluster together like this," (pointing to the screen) "it is not good."

As the doctor was explaining this to me, tears started rolling down my face and the nice nurse standing behind me gave me some tissue. I realized the nurse already knew that I would need the tissue. While the doctor was explaining this, in my mind I said, "He's telling me that I have breast cancer."

I just could not believe what I was hearing. Questions raced through my mind. How did I get this? Where did it come from? While the tears were still running down my face, the nurse gave me the name of an oncologist who would tell me what to do next.

This time when I went home, I told my husband what was going on and what the doctors said. This time I was a little scared. My husband hugged me and said, "Rose, it is going to be alright. We believe God for your healing." He began to pray right then and said he would go with me to the next appointment.

My husband and I went to the next appointment together to hear what this oncologist had to say. On the drive there, we talked, but not about this. Later I learned that while driving to the doctor's office we were both thinking the same thing but said nothing. We were both thinking that the doctor would tell us that I was fine, that they didn't see anything in the x-rays, or that all I needed to do was take some pills to fix this. But that's not at all what the doctor said to us.

This doctor confirmed that I had breast cancer. She looked at the x-ray and confirmed the calcifications in my breast. This time she saw it in two areas of my breast, which meant it was spreading. The doctor said the good news is that it is contained in my breast. She kept talking bluntly and fast, and all I heard was the part about removing my breast. I then repeated her words about removing my breast. The tears started flowing again. My husband interrupted her as she was talking and asked her to slow down and let us get an understanding of what she was saying. He started asking questions and she slowed down and answered his questions. I was still crying, but I was listening. Then she told me that I was lucky. This is a term my husband did not believe in. He told her that we do not believe in luck; instead, we are blessed.

The doctor changed her wording and said I was blessed because I have life. I could continue to live because this cancer was not in my body. She said, "If it were in your body, I would tell you to go home and have a party and drink all the vodka you wanted to. But this cancer is contained in your breast, and you can live." She said the words, "You have breast cancer," but she quickly said, "We can save your life. Breast cancer does not mean you will die if you do as I tell you to."

She then discussed surgery—a mastectomy and reconstruction. She gave me some pamphlets to read and said the office would call me with a date for surgery.

In the pamphlet, it explained how the mastectomy and reconstruction would be done. The name of the procedure was "TRAM Flap." I understood how it was to be done, but I kept thinking of having only one breast. I would have two doctors: one doing the mastectomy and the other doing the reconstruction. The mastectomy meant removing the cancer by cleaning (cutting) out the tissue inside of my breast. The reconstruction meant that the skin on my breast would still be there, and they would fill it with my own flesh, taken from my abdomen area. It would look like I had my own breast. But my mind kept telling me I would have only one breast.

After all this added information, my husband and I were driving back home from this appointment, both completely quiet. It had to settle in our minds; we were still taking this in. I had breast cancer. I kept saying in my mind, "I have breast cancer," in disbelief.

Chapter Four

I remember thinking about the words breast cancer. I thought those words meant death, and I was fearful.

Before we reached home, I told my husband that we would have to tell the kids. We had three children in their twenties and one nine-year-old. We told them (excluding the nine- year-old, who was in school at this time) what the doctor said and that this did not mean death. I would live, but I would have to have surgery. Of course, this was upsetting news. The children did not take it well because, just like me, they thought the words breast cancer meant death.

Our oldest son was hurt, and he was really concerned that I would do what the doctor said to do. Our second son was a little shocked but proceeded to ask questions and asked what I had to do next. Our daughter was not home, but for some reason she called home from work and asked me what we were doing. Now I was a little emotional, and I could not go through the story again. I quickly handed the phone to my oldest son to talk to her. I motioned to him not to tell her now, but to wait until she came home. She felt something was going on, and she hung up the phone and was home in a flash. She took the news hard and cried, but I told her not to cry and explained again what the doctor said about it being contained. She ran out of the house and went for a drive. When she came back, she was better, and we talked some more. Everyone in the house was concerned and said to do what the doctor said so that I could get better.

My husband and I both decided not to tell our nine-year-old yet.

Not My Normal

While waiting for the surgery date, everyone was praying for me: pastors, churches, friends, and family. I remember my oldest sister called me crying about this breast cancer I now had. I told her that I was alright, and she should not worry about me because God would take care of me and take me through this. This time I put my trust in God as I read His Word. God assured me he was the one who healed diseases (Psalm 103:3). He was the one who brought my soul up from the grave and kept me alive (Psalm 30:3). He brings health and cures, and an abundance of peace and truth (Jeremiah 33:6). Jesus healed sickness and disease (Matthew 9:35). If He healed me, I would be healed, if He saved me, I would be saved; He is my praise (Jeremiah 17:14)!

God did keep me. He kept my mind from feeling sorry for myself and worrying about this. He kept me in good spirits. I remember lying in bed one day saying to myself, "You should be crying right now because you have breast cancer." But I was not crying, nor was I worried. I know that the Lord did this for me because according to His Word He said, "And the peace of God, which passeth all understanding, shall keep your hearts and minds through Christ Jesus" (Philippians 4:7).

I read all the healing scriptures I could find in the Bible and read them every day. One day as I was studying the Word about healing, somehow I got on scriptures about dying. I read that the Lord said, "Precious in the sight of the LORD is the death of his saints" (Psalm 116:15). I read, "For me to live is Christ, and to die is gain" (Philippians 1:21). And then I read, "Blessed are the dead which die in the Lord from henceforth: Yea, saith the Spirit, that they may rest from their labours; and their works do follow them" (Revelation 14:13).

After reading these verses, I said to the Lord in a questioning and high pitch voice, "Lord, are you trying to tell me that I am going to die?"

I did not know what I was feeling after reading this. I had to deal with the fact that I might die. I thought the Lord was preparing me, showing me how to manage this fact. I finally got to the point where I told the Lord, "If I am going to die, I want to be ready for you, Lord, and I love you no matter what happens."

I had to continue to study the Word of God to get to this point, but I did get there. The Word of God said, "For whether we live, we live unto the Lord; and whether we die, we die unto the Lord: whether we live therefore, or die, we are the Lord's" (Romans 14:8). And when I got to that point, I felt such a relief. I felt like this is what the Lord was waiting for me to say. He wanted me to get to the point that I loved Him even if He did not heal me from breast cancer.

The time came when the doctor's office called with a date for the mastectomy and reconstruction surgery. I did not want to have a mastectomy, but I did want to live.

In the midst of waiting for surgery, a family matter came up that made me cancel my surgery date. At this point, we had moved to Savannah and Malachi was in the fifth grade. I had to go back to New Jersey for the surgery. Several months earlier, I had to go back to New Jersey for doctor appointments and Malachi stayed in Savannah with his dad. Well, his dad had to work, so he would get Malachi up extra early in the morning for school. We had arrangements for Malachi to stay with a friend who offered to help us. That friend would take Malachi to primetime (for early students before school started) and then after school Malachi would go to after school care until our friend picked him up. He stayed with our friend until his father picked him up and they went home. Malachi told me that he did not want to do that again. I think it all was too much for him. He pleaded with me not to leave him again and all I could hear was the cry of my child. This broke my heart, so I decided to postpone my surgery.

After I made this decision, I called the doctor's office to speak with the doctor. She was out of town on vacation and could not be reached. The nurse asked if she could help me. I told the nurse that I was postponing the surgery. The nurse got a little concerned and said, "Are you sure about this? We do not recommend you do this. Can you wait until the doctor comes back?" I told her I could not wait, and that I would call back to get another date for my surgery.

Well, when the doctor came back from her vacation, she called me and blasted me for postponing the surgery. She said, "I am trying to save your life; you cannot do this." She calmed down and told me to set up an appointment to have x-rays done again and not to cancel this appointment.

After the x-rays were done, I came into the office to see the doctor. She showed me how the cancer had spread in my breast. She told me that I could not cancel surgery again, and that she was trying to save my life.

Chapter Four

While I was waiting for the new date of the surgery, I noticed that I had lost a little weight; it just fell off. I remember feeling fatigued, and for some reason my arms would hurt when making my bed or raising my arms. I also remember combing my hair, and it was coming out. I prayed and asked the Lord not to let my hair fall out. After a while, I was combing my hair one day and saw the hair in my comb, but at the same time the Lord allowed my hair to grow. I thanked the Lord for that, because he gave me peace and let me know that I could ask Him anything: "Be careful for nothing; but in every thing by prayer and supplication with thanksgiving let your requests be made known unto God" (Philippians 4:6).

Also, I remember everyone was praying for me. People were sending cards and gifts to encourage me. A gentleman from our church sent me about six books loaded with information on breast cancer, and the ladies from our church made me a prayer blanket with healing Scriptures on it. It was so sweet and caring of them, and it made me feel loved.

I remember my oldest son was getting married and set the date for his wedding on October 15. At this time, Malachi, my husband, and I were in the process of moving to Savannah. My husband had already left earlier and now Malachi and I were moving our last items to Savannah and Calvin Jr. and is bride-to-be drove us down. To cut down on traveling back to New Jersey for the wedding and then the surgery, which we found out was now scheduled for November 15, Calvin Jr. and his bride-to-be changed their wedding date to November 5.

It was only a three-week difference, but it meant a lot to me. He wanted to get married before I had the surgery so that I could be there to enjoy seeing my firstborn child getting married. I had a great time at the wedding and was so proud of my son and his new bride.

Finally, the day came for the mastectomy and reconstruction surgery. My husband and Malachi were there with me, and friends and family came with me to the hospital. It was a great feeling having them there to support me and knowing that people cared enough about me to take time to come to the hospital. I remember praying and asking the Lord to heal me because I did not want to have this surgery. He had healed Clarence's ears and saved him from surgery, so I knew God could heal me too. But that was not His plan for me.

Having one breast removed was not a good feeling or even a good thought. I truly dreaded this surgery. I could not imagine me with one breast, but this was going to save my life. When they called my name, Calvin and I went in the back with the nurse. While we were standing there, I again told my husband that I wish I did not have to do this. He said that it would be alright, and that this was going to save my life. The nurse came in to prepare me for surgery, so Calvin gave me a kiss and left the room.

The mastectomy and reconstruction lasted six hours, I was told. From there I was placed in recovery until a hospital room was available. I was in the hospital for three days. On the first morning after the surgery, the nurse had me up early and had me walking. I remember the pain. I also remember how pleasant and attentive the nurses were. I thanked the Lord for that too. When the doctors came to see me, they said that I was doing surprisingly well.

The day came for me to go home. After I got home, I started checking out what was done to me in surgery. My right breast was covered with bandages. But I looked until I saw my breast was still there—at least it looked like my breast. There was a tube on the side of my breast which collected the fluid and needed to be drained.

The doctor had scheduled a nurse to come to my house the next day after I was released from the hospital. The nurse changed my bandages and drained the fluid. She commented on the great job the doctors did. When she was finished, she began asking me questions and I answered them. She also explained to me how to change the bandages and drain the fluid. She said, "You don't need me, do you?" I answered, "No, I can do this myself."

After the nurse left, I was feeling so well that I decided to go downstairs and make myself breakfast. Everyone was so surprised I was up and trying to make breakfast. I am so grateful to God for life.

Eventually, I wrote a nice thank you letter to the nursing staff at the hospital on the floor where I stayed. I also wrote letters to the doctors for their awesome work and to my church and other churches, thanking them for their prayers and kindness.

One day, I was thinking about all that took place. I never stopped to think about what God could do. I only thought that if God could heal me, I would not have to go through the operation. But God did something else. He brought me through the operation with such a quick healing it was amazing. I really thought the whole thing was going to be a mess. Even the visiting home nurse said that I was doing so well that I did not need her.

While I was thinking, I realized if I had not kept my mammogram appointment that cold day, I would have waited an entire year for the next mammogram appointment, thinking that everything was alright with my body. By that time, the cancer would have spread in my body, and who knows where I would be today.

After the surgery, I had to take the medicine called tamoxifen for the next five years. Tamoxifen helps to prevent the chances of the recurrence of cancer. I am now going into my nineteenth year of being cancer free. I am grateful for the doctors that attended to me, and I am so grateful to God for life. God has a plan.

Chapter Five
First Lady

When I was growing up, I remember telling the Lord that I never wanted to be a first lady in the church. But years later I found myself in that position when my husband became a pastor. God is God, and He knows us, and He knows what He has in store for us: "But as it is written, Eye hath not seen, nor ear heard, neither have entered into the heart of man, the things which God hath prepared for them that love him" (1 Corinthians 2:9). He has our future in His hands, and He knows what He has called us to do.

I was always afraid of the idea of being a first lady. I thought that she would have to look a certain way, that she would have to act a certain way and that she would have to do certain things in church. But I have learned that God has called me to be no one else except me, to spend time with Him in prayer, to study His Word, and to follow His instructions (Deuteronomy 11:1).

When I was growing up, I attended several different churches. In one of those churches, I remember the first lady had sadness in her eyes. Even though she smiled at times, I could see on her face that she was unhappy. Her unhappiness stuck in my heart, and it played a part in me not wanting to become a first lady. I thought being a first lady was hard. I realized that as a first lady people watch you, analyze you, watch your facial expressions, and listen to your choice of words among other things.

First Lady

People think because you are the first lady that you have everything you want. But building the lives of people is not an easy job. My husband worked hard to build and teach people the Word of God. He gave up his time and his money to do what the Lord called him to do. And when he makes sacrifices that means I also make sacrifices. People think you have money and can do whatever you want but it is the opposite; you don't have money and you cannot do whatever you want to do. God called us to be an example and to let our life shine so others can see that it is possible to live for Him (Matthew 5:16). Because you are a first lady it is not about spending money to look good. There is nothing wrong with looking good, but that should not be on the top of our list. We have a standard to uphold for God. We have a dedication to God to live a life pleasing

1996

to Him, and we are called by God to teach His Word and to win souls for His kingdom.

There was a time in my life when I felt and heard myself say, "God called my husband to pastor—not me." I felt that I had no role in this; that I was just my husband's wife. But as time passed, I learned that being the first lady meant that I did have a role in this, and that I am a part of this. I am a helper to my husband, and I have a responsibility to do what the Lord has called me to do and be who He has called me to be. I realized that I represented God and my husband.

When my husband became a pastor, our children were still little. We had one preschooler, one in kindergarten, and one second grader. Taking care of our little ones was a full-time responsibility. They were my priority and ministry.

I remember when our children were at the age where I could get them all dressed and ready to go to church on time. Before this, I would dress the two boys first and then my daughter. The boys would stay clean and not rip anything, but if I got my daughter dressed first, she would rip her tights or get her clothes dirty. Then I would have to take more time to change her clothes. So, I started dressing her after I dressed the boys. And I made her sit on the bed in front of me while I was getting dressed until we were ready to leave for church. We did not have Sunday school back then, so we did not have to leave the house too early on Sunday morning.

As time passed, I would wonder what I could do to be of help to my husband in the church. Usually, back in the nineties at least, the first lady had the talent of either singing or playing the piano. I had neither of these talents, and I did not know what I was going to do in the ministry.

Well, again, God had a purpose and a plan. My husband decided that we needed to do something with all the children at church, so we started a Sunday school class for them. I became a Sunday school teacher for little children. I enjoyed doing this for many years. I was teaching little ones first, and then as the years passed, I began teaching teenagers. I found my niche.

Years later, the church needed an adult Sunday school teacher, and they were asking for a volunteer for this position. I was happy and comfortable doing what I was doing, and I was afraid to do adult Sunday school class. In the meeting as they asked for a volunteer to be an adult Sunday school teacher, a young lady who was a new Christian said she would do it. I thought this was not good, because she was a new Christian who needed to grow in the things of God and learn the Word of God for herself.

My heart kept nudging me to take the position as adult Sunday school teacher. But I was afraid that I couldn't do it, that I didn't know enough of the Word of God, and that the adults might ask questions I wouldn't be able to answer. But I felt the nudging of the Lord to take this position, so I said I would do it. It's amazing how the Lord pulled me out of my comfortable space.

The young lady who was a new Christian and had volunteered to teach the class had no complaints. She understood when I, the pastor's wife, said I would be the new adult Sunday school teacher. She also attended the Sunday school class every Sunday and was eager to learn. She was a blessing.

Teaching Sunday school pushed me to study the Bible more. Soon I found out that I loved it and that this is what the Lord called me to do. Later, my husband asked me to teach our new members class, and eventually, I also taught women's Bible study lessons and was speaking at our women's services.

Some years later, my husband asked me to teach midweek Bible study. And years after that, I had appointments for other women's services outside of our church. I loved it, and the Lord taught me so much. Sometimes in my life's situations I noticed I was either going through what the lesson was teaching or would go through it later.

God is amazing, and he has a plan for our lives even if

2021

we don't know it yet. Ephesians 2:10 says, "For we are his workmanship, created in Christ Jesus unto good works, which God hath before ordained that we should walk in them." Even though I felt that I could not teach adult Sunday school class, the Lord knew I could do it with His help, and the Lord also knew what I needed.

Through fellowshipping with other churches, I met several other first ladies. In our conversations, I noticed that as pastor's wives, we kept a lot of things to ourselves. Some of us did not have close friends. We had friends who were more like acquaintances because some first ladies made it known that their husbands had a large church and a large membership. And because some of us did not want our husbands to look small in the eyes of others simply because they did not have a large church membership, we learned that we could not talk to everybody. And yes, you must be careful who you tell your business to. But this also put us in a certain frame of mind that kept us from drawing truly close to one another.

I remember thinking to myself that I would not allow this big church membership attitude to make me feel less than them. I believed in my husband, and I believed he had a calling on his life. I stood beside him not just because he could preach the Lord's Word, but because he lived what he preached. I was so proud of him for following the directions of the Lord.

There was a time when the Lord was leading me to help bring other first ladies together for fellowship and lunch. I felt like I was going to lead a first ladies ministry. I finally did gather about five to six women, all pastors' wives, for lunch and fellowship. We met and had fun talking. The ladies all said they enjoyed themselves and wanted to do it again. But before we could do it again my husband and I decided to move to Savannah, GA to take over our other church where the pastor resigned.

I remember my husband and I went to dinner with a new pastor we had met and become friendly with. This pastor was female, and I was sitting there listening to them talk about church stuff. Usually conversations with pastors were between my husband and them. My husband began talking about how he is trying to live a healthy life—eating healthy and going to the gym to work out. As she was listening, she suddenly turned to me and said, "Well, Rosemary, what do you like to do?"

I knew she was asking me about what I personally like to do. I was not sure how to answer that. I had to think fast. In my mind, I was asking myself, "What do I like to do?

God has our future in His hands and He knows what He has called us to do.

What do I like?" The first thing I came up with was shopping, which I love but don't get to do too often. At that moment, I realized I didn't know what I liked for myself. I felt lost, but I kept cool and calm and gave an answer. But that question haunted me for several days, and this was not the first time.

In many years of being a mother, a wife, and working in the church, life gets busy. You can forget about you, what you want, who you are, and what you like to do for yourself. I had to find me. I learned that in the midst of doing God's work, we must take care of ourselves. We must take care of our bodies and our minds while taking care of our marriage and families. We must take some time to read a book, relax, see a movie, take a walk or drive, or just be at home alone or whatever other things we like to do. We are taking care of everyone else: our children, our husbands. We are playing our part in church, being role models and examples to others, helping others, and praying for others. We need to do things just for us, that make us feel good about ourselves and renew our minds, remembering to always pray and ask for God's guidance and direction. We need to make sure that we are emotionally "Casting down imaginations, and every high thing that exalteth itself against the knowledge of God, and bringing into captivity every thought to the obedience of Christ" (2 Corinthians 10:5). Physical health is also important: "Beloved, I wish above all things that thou mayest prosper and be in health, even as thy soul prospereth" (3 John 2). Above all, we must be spiritually healthy: "But grow in grace, and in the knowledge of our

Lord and Saviour Jesus Christ. To him be glory both now and for ever. Amen" (2 Peter 3:18).

I know this now because I experienced this myself. I found myself drained and unhappy. I was doing the things I needed to do for my family and for the church, but I was unhappy. I realized that I was not doing anything for myself, and I felt dissatisfied on the inside. So, there I was asking the Lord for help again. I love the Lord because He said that I can "come boldly unto the throne of grace, that we may obtain mercy, and find grace to help in the time of need" (Hebrews 4:16).

From here I started reminding myself to take some time for me. I started walking, reading, and doing some other things for myself. With the help of the Lord and His guidance, I got through this. After many seasons of both sickness and health in many areas, I know that my emotional, physical, and spiritual well-being were a part of God's plan and purpose!

Chapter Six

Pain

There was a time on my journey of life that I cried every day. I had let one negative thought grow big—the thought of not being enough, not being educated enough, not finishing college, and not making enough money. I let it consume my mind and I believed it. And that grew into depression.

At that time, I was working in the church office. I would drive my youngest son to school and then come back to the church and go into the sanctuary to pray—to cry out to God for help—before going upstairs to work in the office.

I also worked for the church day care, and one day I had to cover a teacher's class while she went to lunch. The children were down for a nap. While I was sitting there, I started to think about my life situation, and I got a little emotional. Tears started rolling down my face. One of the children was watching me—I thought they were all asleep—and asked me why I was crying. I replied, "I am not crying. Now you need a nap. Go to sleep." As I was sitting there thinking, I asked the Lord why things were not the way I wanted them to be.

Things were not lined up the way I felt they should be. I felt like some things should be a certain way, and like I should have obtained certain things by that time in my life. And there I was, feeling a little down and putting myself down because my life was not where I thought it should be.

Chapter Six

Life brings its disappointments and hurts, and sometimes it felt like God was just not hearing me. But deep down inside my heart I knew there was a God and I thanked Him for His grace, mercy, and unconditional love.

Later I learned that without trials in my life, I would not be able to help someone else or have a testimony that the Lord can and will bring us through the tough times. As Isaiah 41:10 says, "Fear thou not; for I am with thee: be not dismayed; for I am thy God: I will strengthen thee; yea, I will help thee; yea, I will uphold thee with the right hand of my righteousness."

I remember telling the Lord that I had cried so much that there could not be any water left in my body. But I was wrong; the next day the water came on again.

Pain and heartache are part of life. I truly thank God for helping me through all the tough times.

I have learned from my experiences that you must believe in yourself, study the Word of God, and trust Him with your life.

In that season of depression, I felt that I could not tell anyone about this—not anyone who knew me. I felt that I had no one I could talk to with the assurance that what I said would stay confidential. I remember being so full on the inside. I knew it was the negative thought that got me into depression, and I needed to get that thought out of my head. I needed to be free of this. I was always praying and asking God for help.

One day the Lord sent someone that I could talk to that did not know me or my family. I had seen this woman many times, but I did not know her. There was something about her that caught my attention. I would see her during work at my corporate job as I walked to the cafeteria and rode up and down the elevator. One day this lady got in the elevator and said hello. We were the only two people in the elevator. I said hello, and we just started talking. As we stepped off the elevator, we were still talking, but I was being cautious about what I was saying. But then I felt it was okay to talk to her—like God had given me the okay. I even felt like the Lord set this up just for me. Because I was so full on the inside, I started talking and crying all at the same time, and everything kind of gushed out of my mouth so fast. The lady said, "It's okay, I understand." So, I continued to talk, and she listened. At the end, she said that she would be praying for me and that she believed the Lord allowed us to meet one another on this elevator. I was so grateful for that, and I knew it was from God.

Another time this happened to me again after church when this lady came to speak to me. She was someone that I kind of trusted. She just said, "Are you alright?" and before I knew it, words started pouring out of my mouth so fast it sounded like gibberish. I then apologized to her, and she said, "It's okay, I understand." I didn't share too much. I shared that I was going through a tough time right now and I needed prayer. She said that she would be praying for me and if I needed to talk, I could call her. Because I was married to a pastor, I felt like I couldn't or shouldn't share my problems with anyone, especially a member of our church.

Well, this thing—this depression—went on. I was able to do all the things I needed to do to take care of my home and family, but on the inside, I was miserable. I remember going to church and I could not open my mouth to praise the Lord. I had to praise the Lord in my heart because I could not speak. I remember the tears flowing down my face because I needed help with this. Everyone thought I was crying tears of praise, but I was crying out to the Lord from my heart for help.

Even at home I couldn't open my mouth to praise the Lord. I cried out to God in my heart and mind. I kept calling Jesus in my heart. Every chance I got—even when cooking, cleaning, working, checking homework for my children, ironing, and everything else—I called Jesus because I needed help.

My parents lived in Florida at this time, and my mom came to visit. As soon as she stepped into the house and said hello, she said, "What's wrong, Rose?" and of course I replied, "Nothing." "Nothing" was always my reply. I don't know why, but it was just much easier to say "Nothing" when asked what's wrong. My husband also asked me what's wrong and immediately I replied "Nothing." Looking back on this, I needed someone. I needed him to really press me about what was wrong. After a long visit, my mom was getting ready to leave for Florida. She said to me, "I know there's something wrong even if you won't tell me." I love her for that.

Well, this depression and crying went on, and I kept calling Jesus in my heart. I would think about this depression—this bondage—and I wanted to be free of it. I wanted to be free inside my heart and in my mind. So, in my mind and in my heart, I would just say, "Jesus, Jesus, I need help. Jesus, I need your help." I would constantly ask the Lord for help.

I now understood the saying about feeling like a crab in a basket. I would do good, and feel better, and I felt like I was progressing and climbing out of the basket that held me captive. And then I would fall back into the basket. But I kept on trying. I kept calling Jesus in my heart until one day the Lord allowed me to be free. This sounds easy, but it took me some time to get out of this. With the help of the Lord, I made it. I got free of this depression and finally climbed out of the basket. The Word of God says to "Cast thy burden upon the LORD, and he shall sustain thee: he shall never suffer the righteous to be moved" (Psalm 55:22). God is a great God.

God helped me to understand that I must be careful of what thoughts I allow to enter my mind: "Finally, brethren, whatsoever things are true, whatsoever things are honest, whatsoever things are just, whatsoever things are pure, whatsoever things are lovely, whatsoever things are of good report; if there be any virtue, and if there be any praise, think on these things" (Philippians 4:8).

Sometimes you cannot help what thoughts pop up into your mind, but you can cast out the wrong ones and not let them take root in your heart.

After this, Philippians 4:8 became my nightly recital. Several years later, the same thought that started this popped into my mind, and I was instantly reminded by the Holy Spirit that this is how I got into depression before. I immediately pleaded the blood of Jesus, thanked the Lord for understanding, and changed my thinking.

I was glad God had given me the understanding to overcome negative thoughts, because more pain and loss were coming.

Chapter Six

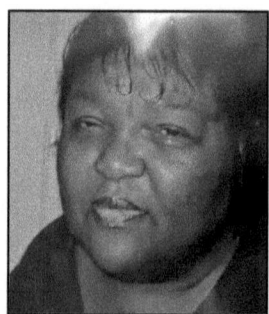

My late younger sister Kathy

On June 24, 2016, I lost my sister Kathy. She and her family were traveling to our family reunion—the first one she would have attended. On their way there, they had a car accident. The car flipped upside down. The ambulance and police came and got everyone out. They went to the hospital, and she was gone. I did not attend that year, but my sister Carolyn called me and told me about the car accident. She then said, "Kathy is gone." I asked her what she was saying, and Carolyn told me again that Kathy was gone. I asked her what she was talking about several times and then it sank in. My sister Kathy had passed away. I just couldn't believe it. She was the first of my siblings to pass away. I have five siblings; I am the second child, and Kathy was the fifth child.

Two years later, on August 30, 2018, my father passed away. I remember getting a phone call from Carolyn, my oldest sister, saying Daddy is going to the hospital because he was having trouble breathing. He had been to the hospital for this same reason several times before. Daddy had to be feeling extremely sick, because he called Carolyn and told her he wanted to go to the hospital, which is something he would not normally do. When I got to the hospital, the nurses were setting him up on oxygen, so we could not go into the room. But about thirty minutes later, we were able to go in and see him. This reminded me of several other times when he was hospitalized in the past.

We could see he was struggling to breathe, and we were all praying for him. After we had been there for several hours, I realized that my mom had not eaten all day during this situation. My brother-in-law and I took my mom to get something to eat. She was a diabetic, something she kept denying. When we came back to the hospital, we heard our name being called over the loudspeaker, so we went to the office window. They told us to go through the doors and into the waiting room, and the nurse would come to speak to us. My heart told me what was going on, but I told myself to stop thinking and wait to hear what the nurse had to say. But when we came into the room, Carolyn was crying—really crying—and I knew then what the nurse was going to tell us. At that time, the nurse entered the room and told us that my father had passed away, and she explained to us what happened. I was keeping an eye on my mother as she was standing there listening. I was watching her because if she passed out or broke down in tears, I would be there to hold her. I was just stunned. I couldn't believe this.

The next year on December 11, 2019, we lost my oldest sister, my friend, Carolyn. She was dealing with breast cancer. I watched her get sick, then get better to the point where she was sitting up talking to us and looking at her cell phone. Then I watched her being put in a nursing home and getting worse, being sent back to the hospital, and then going into a coma and passing away. We were all heartbroken.

In 2020, the COVID-19 pandemic hit the world. On February 1, 2021, my brother-in-law, my sister Carolyn's husband, got sick while he was out of town. He went to the emergency room because he was not feeling well and was sent home. They said he did not have COVID. The next day he was still feeling awful, so he went back to the emergency room, and he never came home. Because he was out of town, a friend of his called his daughters to let them know. The doctor said that my brother-in-law passed away from COVID even though the first time he went to the emergency room they told him that he did not have COVID.

My late older sister and brother-in-law Carolyn and Phillip

Pain

I was shocked and trying to keep my mind. I was feeling terrible and asking God what was going on. Why were my loved ones leaving here? My heart was hurting, and I didn't know if I could take another loss. But Psalm 28:7 tells me that "the Lord is my strength and my shield; my heart trusted in him, and I am helped: therefore my heart greatly rejoiceth; and with my song will I praise him."

When Carolyn was with us, she lived close to my parents, and after our father passed away, she looked after our mother. Carolyn moved our mother in with her. But when Carolyn passed away, my youngest sister Tammy and I had to look after and take care of our mother. We tried and tried to convince her to live with one of us, but she wanted to live by herself. So, she lived by herself for a year, and we would take her to appointments, grocery stores, shopping, out to dinner, and for drives in the car. Then she decided to move in with Tammy—she said my house had too many stairs. After we got all her things moved into Tammy's house, and she was settled, she decided to spend a week with me because I had to take her to a couple of doctor's appointments.

Usually, she would get up early and get herself dressed and sit in the chair waiting for me to get up. That morning, we were supposed to go back for my mother's second COVID shot, but she was not feeling well. The next day I checked on her, but she was still not feeling well. So, on the third morning, I asked her how she felt. She replied that she didn't feel well and couldn't get out of bed. I decided to call the ambulance because I was scared.

The ambulance came, and the paramedics asked a lot of questions and checked her out. I gave the paramedics all her medical information, which included the fact that about two months ago we found out that she had lung cancer. The paramedic talked as if he was not going to take her to the hospital, because he said that her symptoms were normal symptoms for lung cancer. I told them that I was scared and wanted to find out what was wrong with my mother.

They took her to the hospital, and I called Tammy to let her know. Because of COVID, we could not go into the hospital because Tammy and I both had colds. Tammy and I called the hospital to find out how she was doing. We talked to the nurse and then to the doctor. We asked if we could talk to our mother. They said we could not talk to her then, but they would set up a time the next day to Facetime us. When they Facetimed us, we could see she was sick, but she recognized our voices as we talked to her.

My mother was in the hospital for a little over a week, and we talked with the nurse and the doctor regularly. The doctor told us that she had COVID and was very sick. As we continued to talk, I felt that he was trying to tell us that my mom was at the end. I did not say anything to Tammy because I was too afraid to let those thoughts go through my mind. After we hung up the phone, the nurse called us on Facetime, and we were able to see my mother. She was not doing well at all.

On April 6, 2021, we again talked with the nurse and the doctor, and they said that my mother was doing the same as the last time we talked. We asked some questions, and we hung up the phone. Within an hour, they called us back that day to let us know she had passed away.

My heart was hurting. I could not believe my mother was gone. Tammy and I were quiet for a moment then said we needed to call our brother and sister to let them know. Tammy called our brother, and I called our other sister. When I spoke to my sister, I had to repeat those words, "Our mother is gone," several times because she could not hear or comprehend what I was saying. After I hung up the phone, I felt like I was in a daze. I was in disbelief. I was numb. I did not know what to say or do. It felt as if everything stood still—no movement, no sound, no nothing. The doctor told us that my mom passed away from COVID, not from lung cancer. This happened two months after my brother-in-law passed away.

My late father and mother

I have learned that the Lord will take care of us and help us through all things. I have learned that He will bring us through the tough times and that the Lord tells us to bring our burdens to Him (Matthew 11:28). Through reading the Word of God, I have learned that the Lord will comfort us (Matthew 5:4), He will give us peace

(Philippians 4:7); and He will give us strength (Psalm 119:28). Believing in God's Word brought me these things.
Even in this, God had a plan.

Chapter Seven
Life as a Mother

I have learned that the Lord gives us the strength and courage to be able to handle the responsibilities of life. Included in those responsibilities is raising our children. It takes strength, patience, focus, determination, and calling on the Lord for guidance. It takes a lot to be a mother, and we need the Lord's help. He tells us that we can do all things through Christ (Philippians 4:13).

I am reminded of something that my mother wrote years ago about being a mother:

It Makes a Difference When You Are a Mother
by Inez Nealy

It takes loving, sharing, and caring
It takes reasoning, disagreeing, agreeing, discipline, disappointment, and punishment

It makes a difference when you are a mother
It takes wisdom, knowledge, and understanding
It takes teaching, accepting, confessing, and pressing

It makes a difference when you are a mother
It takes fulfillment, enjoyment, responsibility, encouragement, concentration, communication, trusting, believing, and receiving

It makes a difference when you are a mother
It takes determination and continuation

I know because I am a mother

What a special role and responsibility God has given us as mothers. It is a twenty-four-hour and seven-day-a-week position, with no time off. As mothers, we have a very important job—to raise our children to become great and godly people: "And all thy children shall be taught of the LORD; and great shall be the peace of thy children" (Isaiah 54:13).

As mothers, we have our hands full, because from the time they are born, we are their everything. We nurture them, guide them, and protect them until they are old enough to take care of themselves. We feed them, dress them, rock and sing them to sleep, and bathe them when they are still little. We teach them how to pee straight and sit on the toilet, and we become their playmate and their sing-along partner. We are their doctor and their nurse, their English and math teacher, their speech therapist, their game partner, their referee, and their taxi. We teach them manners, how to be respectful, and so much more.

I remember one day when they were toddlers, all three of my children (Malachi was not born yet) asked for a glass of water. Even the Word of God said, "Whosoever shall give to drink unto one of these little ones a cup of cold water only in the name of the disciple, verily I say unto you, he shall in no wise lose his reward" (Matthew 10:42). There was nothing wrong with asking for water, but they asked one at a time, right behind each other. One asked for water, I got up and gave him a glass of water. As soon as I sat down, the next one asked for a glass of water, and soon as I sat down again the third child asked for a glass of water. I remember thinking, "Lord, I'm never going to get out of this," meaning I would be busy for a long, long time. At that moment, I was a little overwhelmed and felt like my life did not belong to me any longer.

I just felt tired and stressed. I couldn't even read and study the Bible until the children went to sleep. I would say things like, "I am tired," and "I feel stressed out." The more I said these things, the more I felt them. I had to learn to stop grumbling and complaining about all I had to do and start enjoying my time with my children while I still had them with me. I had to start enjoying where I was in life. The more I complained, the more I felt stressed. In reading the Word of God, I found a scripture that said the Lord will comfort my soul (Psalm 94:19). I thanked God for His Word.

As parents, we are responsible for teaching our children about right and godly living and to watch out for wrong things. There are times we can see things that our children can't see. For instance, at certain ages there are things on television they should not see or hear, and we must use our judgment on what things are sending the wrong messages. We are there to protect them. Because parents have lived longer and experienced more than their children, they know what is ahead of them or what is not good for them. I am not saying that as parents we know everything or that we always get it right, because we don't; but with the help of the Lord, we must do all we know to do to help guide and protect our children.

If we continue to do our job, one day we will see the results. When they become adults and we see they are good people making good choices and doing the right thing with their lives, we will become proud parents. I used to tell my children that I wanted them to grow up to be good productive citizens in society.

Raising children was especially important to me. It may be because my mother was home with me and my siblings growing up. But whatever it was, I have always felt a great responsibility to raise the children the Lord gave me and my husband. I remember giving birth to each of them and looking at their little faces, then feeling that great responsibility. I really felt this way each time I gave birth.

When I was growing up, I saw fathers who were pastors neglecting their children because they were busy doing church work. I put in my mind that I would never let this happen to my children. I was determined not to let my children be neglected. I wanted to be there for them and guide them.

As I look back, I tried to catch everything going on in their lives that needed correction and guidance. My thought was if something was wrong, or they were going through some struggle, I could help them before it was too late. I know I missed some things, but I tried. I know life can be hard, but I wanted them to have the tools to make it in this life. As I was instructed in Proverbs 22:6: "Train up a child in the way he should go: and when he is old, he will not depart from it."

While they were growing up, we would pray and read scriptures together, and in my prayer time, I would pray for them. But I wanted them to know that they could also pray for themselves. I wanted them to know that they could call on the Lord for whatever they needed.

I remember telling the Lord to let them be like their daddy: a strong, ambitious, and determined person that would not give up and not be a follower. Today, they all are like their daddy. They are all strong, ambitious, and determined people who love the Lord, and they keep pushing for better.

Raising children is so important. We, as parents, are raising and teaching the next generation that will make changes and better this world. They will be role models for others.

What we teach our children and how we do it is important. We teach them by example, because the things they see you do, they will do. And they do watch you and hear what you say even when you think they are not listening.

I also want my children to serve the Lord and teach their children to do the same. As parents we can direct them and teach them diligently about the Lord, which we are instructed to do according to the Word of God (Deuteronomy 6:7), but one day they will have to make the decision to serve the Lord for themselves.

I hear young parents say that they will not raise and discipline their children the same way their parents did them. I understand that some things our parents taught us will change. But disciplining children is a must! The Bible tells us if we do not discipline our children, we do not love them (Proverbs 13:24). Why? Because if we do not teach them right from wrong, we show lack of concern for their character development and their life. The method of disciplining can change, but parents must discipline. We do not love them if we allow them to grow up feeling like the world revolves around them and there are no consequences for their actions. We will be setting them up for failure and a hard life.

Disciplining children teaches guidance and right from wrong; it brings structure into their lives. It helps them make good choices. It helps them to learn how to be honest, how to not be influenced by others who are doing the wrong thing, and how to make their own decisions.

As a mother I didn't always get it right and there were times I was fearful—times I didn't have an answer. Despite this, it was still my responsibility to keep trying to give my children direction. I have learned that I can go to God about everything and so I would pray and ask the Lord for guidance. The Word of God says that I can ask and will receive, seek and I will find, and knock and it will be opened to me (Matthew 7:7).

As the children were growing up, there were times I could not tell which child was telling me the truth and which one was not. One time when they were little, I gave them three cookies for their snack. One of them or all of them decided they wanted more, and they got them. When I came downstairs, I saw the evidence they left behind and asked them who got more cookies. None of them would answer and I couldn't tell which one did it. I said to myself, what do I do now? I told them that they all would be in trouble if they did not tell me the truth. Clarence said, "I did it." When something happened Clarence would always confess first, even if he didn't do it. I did not believe him, so they were all in trouble.

I was fearful when the boys were fifteen and sixteen, and I was still trying to hold on to them. I used to drive them everywhere, and then I started letting them walk to places by themselves. My sister was shocked when she saw Calvin Jr. and Clarence walking home from the basketball court several blocks down the street from our house late in the evening. I was learning to let go of them and allow them to grow up.

I was fearful when Clarence asked me if he could go to the mall with some friends in a car. I decided to let him go but everyone in the car—girls and boys—had to get out and come introduce themselves to me. I was learning to let go.

My husband told me that I must give our children some space because they were not little anymore; they were growing up and I could not treat them like babies. This broke my heart, but he was right. I had to allow them to grow up because I wanted them to be strong men.

I was fearful when Tabitha went to college in another state. I would not be there to protect her and guide her. Again, my husband stepped in and said, "Rose, we have taught her well. We have instilled good things into her. She will be ok. We now must trust that she will make right decisions."

I also remember when Malachi wanted to go to football camp. I was a little fearful of that because he was not allowed to use the cell phone to call home. That meant I would not hear from him at all and would not know how he was doing or if something happened. But I let him go because I was allowing him to grow up.

I learned that at this stage in our children's lives I had to trust God to take care of them and to use all that they have been taught. No, it is not easy being a mother because there comes a time you must let go and allow your children to grow up and make their own decisions. And as a mother

I will continue to pray for them and give them advice when I can.

My husband and I are proud of our children. They are not perfect, and they may not do everything the way we would like them to, but we are proud of them. We thank the Lord for using them to spread God's Word in preaching, in singing, in music, and in living it. We thank God for them making the choice to serve the Lord.

I know they have had some tough times themselves, and I know life is not always simple and easy. Life has a lot of scary moments and circumstances. But even they had to learn how to give it all to the Lord and allow Him to guide them.

Although our children are all grown, I still say a prayer for them and our grandchildren. I even pray for our great-grandchildren who are not here yet. I wear the badge of a proud mother with honor and gratefulness, and we thank the Lord for what he has done in the lives of our children.

As mothers, we spend half of our lives raising children, and the other half of our life enjoying our children as adults.

My husband has said to me many times, "You are a blessed woman. God has blessed your womb with children who are preachers, musicians, songwriters, praise and worship leaders, and singers."

I am reminded of Proverbs 31:28, which says, "Her children arise up, and call her blessed; her husband also, and he praiseth her."

I am a blessed woman, and God had a purpose and a plan for my life and for my family's life.

Life as a Mother

Calvin Jr., Tabitha, Clarence, Malachi. The Lord has allowed me to see my children as adults. I am so proud of them.

Chapter Eight
God's Care

I have experienced some life situations where the Lord just blew my mind. My situations may seem like insignificant issues, but the Lord let me know that He is concerned with whatever is concerning me. Nothing is too hard for God (Jeremiah 32:17), and nothing is impossible with the Lord (Luke 1:37). I know God cares about me and my issues. He has proven it to me repeatedly.

In one of my situations, I remember standing in church next to my husband. We were having a special program with a guest speaker. As I was standing there, I was talking to the Lord in my heart—not out loud or with words. Within several minutes, the guest speaker turned to me and said the exact words I had just told the Lord.

In another situation as I got older, I remember going through hot flashes. I was trying to sleep, but the hot flashes got the best of me. I had one leg hanging over the bed, the covers thrown off, and the fan going while the air conditioning was on. I said to God in a desperate voice, "Lord I know there's a reason why you made hot flashes, but can you please lighten this up for me?" Believe it or not, I have not had hot flashes since. I don't know what happened to them, but I thank God for it.

When I was working full time, I had a routine. I would get up at about 4:30 a.m. to pray, read the Word of God, get dressed, get breakfast, and be out of the house by 6:30 a.m. I remember I would stand in my closet to see what I could find to wear. I got so disheartened when every morning I had to hunt for something to put on. I was not able to go shopping, so I had to make do with what I had. I would go to my closet, stand there, and just look, trying to figure out what to wear. I did not want it to look like I was wearing the same outfits repeatedly. One day I was almost late for work because I could not find anything to put on. As I was standing in my closet I said, "Lord, what am I going to wear? It's getting late; I must leave soon." I heard from my heart, take this outfit and match it with a different top. This might sound like nothing, but it was something for me. The Lord told me I could find different outfits if I really looked. Not only did I find different outfits, but it kept me from getting frustrated and from being late for work.

Through life's journey, I have learned that God really does care about me and whatever is going on in my life. The Word of God tells me to be strong, to be of good courage, to have no fear, and to trust that God will not fail me (Deuteronomy 31:6). The Lord also tells me that I can give Him all my burdens and He will sustain me (Psalm 55:22).

So, I do feel favored by God. God has given me a blessed life, a blessed husband, and a blessed family. Even through breast cancer, the Lord kept me and brought me through. He has allowed me to see many things. I now have four beautiful and talented grandchildren, along with one coming soon. I love them and believe the Lord is going to use them to do His will.

I do not want anyone to think that my life was without problems, because life is not like that. Life isn't always easy, but I know from all the things life has presented me is that God is there: "Yea, though I walk through the valley of the shadow of death, I will fear no evil: for thou art with me; thy rod and thy staff they comfort me" (Psalms 23:4). He will bring us through, he will help us, and he will strengthen us through it all. No, we do not have all the answers, but God does. "And it shall come to pass, that

Highly favored by God.

before they call, I will answer; and while they are yet speaking, I will hear" (Isaiah 65:24). Through my experiences I know that God cares for me. He has proven it to me, and I am so grateful to Him.

Here is a final occurrence when God allowed me to see that he has a purpose and a plan for my family. I was sitting in church, enjoying the Lord, and hearing His Word being preached by my oldest son, who was the pastor.

He told the congregation that he heard the Lord say something to him twice, and that he was going to be obedient to God and say it. He then called his son, my grandson, to the front and told him that the Lord said, "You have graduated." He also said that he may not know what this meant yet, but that God would reveal it to him.

Now, while I was watching this, it was not about what he said to my grandson. It was about God showing me His purpose and plan to use my marriage, and to bring forth my children, grandchildren, and generations to come to do His will, to be examples, and to serve Him.

I am not saying that my family is more special than anyone else, because God loves everyone (John 3:16). But I do know that God has a purpose and a plan for my family.

Conclusion

When I look back on how my life played out, I see God's purpose and plan for our family, though I did not see it then.

I think about how things worked out in our lives in a specific pattern. What if that day I had decided not to become his girlfriend? What if I chose not to marry him: in fact, I remember when I was younger telling the Lord that I did not want to marry a musician, a minister, or a pastor. The Lord is so funny because I married all three in my husband. I do believe that God has His hand on our lives. We have been married for forty-five years now and we are still in love, we still enjoy being with each other, and we enjoy serving the Lord together. God has a purpose and a plan!

Today, I feel so blessed and grateful. I feel like Hezekiah Walker's song, "God Favored Me." No, I'm not rich, I'm not famous, but I'm blessed of the Lord. The Lord has taught me many things, and he has kept me through many things. Yes, I went through things. I cried, I experienced hurt and pain, and I had many disappointments. But those things taught me about myself and about God. When I was going through tough times, I did not realize that God was working in my life. But I realized it when He brought me through it and showed me that He cares for me.

I have learned that struggles and things we go through also strengthen us, build us up, and teach us to trust the Lord (1 Peter 5:10). I have learned that God is always

Conclusion

there, and he will never leave us (Deuteronomy 31:8). God never said he would keep us from the hurt, pain, disappointments, and tough times in this life, but he said he would help us through them. The Lord taught me that he really does care about me. One of my favorite Scriptures is 1 Peter 5:7: "Casting all your care upon him; for he careth for you."

Nothing is too little or too big for God. He sees all that we go through and he will help us, he will guide us, he will strengthen us, and he will care for us.

I want all women to know that God does have a purpose and a plan for you and your family. You may not see it, you may not feel it, but God is always working.

Three generations of God's purpose. God has a plan!

About the Author

Rosemary Singleton attended The Cittone Institute for Secretarial Science. She was the First Lady of Victory Revival Temple Ministries located in Perth Amboy, NJ and Living Faith Worship Church located in Savannah, Ga for a total of thirty-six years. Her oldest son is now the pastor of Revive Church Savannah (formerly Living Faith). Mrs. Singleton and her husband, Bishop Calvin N. Singleton, have four grown children and four grandchildren, with one on the way, and are now enjoying retirement as empty nesters. Rosemary enjoys reading, watching movies, sewing, and scrapbooking.